CORVEDALE
and
CASTLES

Marina Oliver

First published in Great Britain by Tudor House, 2006

Printed in Great Britain by WPG, Welshpool

CIP Catalogue entry for this book is available from the British Library

ISBN 0-9530676-4-5

Published in Great Britain by Tudor House,
Coseley House, Munslow, Craven Arms, Shropshire. YS7 9ET
website: www.tudorhouse.net

Local Heritage *initiative*

Corvedale

Corvedale, north east of Ludlow, and situated between Wenlock Edge and the Clee Hills, is one of the loveliest parts of Shropshire. Ellis Peters described it as 'the wide, gracious expanse of Corvedale, farming country with pleasant villages, fine houses, fertile fields'. Simon Jenkins called it a 'glorious sweep of Upper Corvedale, one of Shropshire's secret valleys'.

In 1845 there were plans for a 'mineral railway' through Corvedale, to Craven Arms, and in 1860 another line to Ludlow was proposed, but neither obtained the necessary Parliamentary approval.

Today most people pass swiftly through Corvedale on the B4368. The locals and walkers can take time to explore its secrets and byways and find great enjoyment.

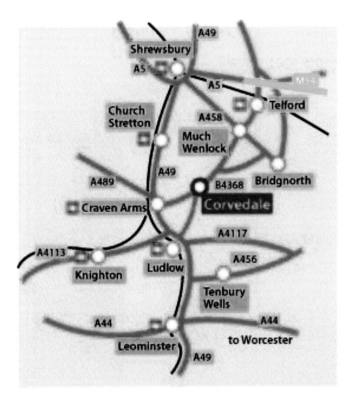

Three Castles Walk and Corvedale

The idea for the walk came from John Farley, a councillor on the Diddlebury Parish Council. He planned the route, obtained permissions from landowners where there were no rights of way, obtained a grant from the Countryside Agency Local Heritage Initiative, and recruited a team to build stiles, clear overgrown paths, and erect waymarkers.

As well as producing the leaflet giving directions, it was decided to publish a book which would give more details about the history and background of the three castles and other buildings on the route, plus nearby relevant places. There is history all around us, and many intriguing snippets of information. Corvedale, sleepy valley as it appears, has had its excitements.

You may wish to take the book with you and read as you go, or read at leisure afterwards. We hope it may tempt you back and give an extra dimension to your enjoyment of the Three Castles Walk.

It is not a comprehensive history of Corvedale, which would occupy a much larger book, but a selection of facts about how people of the past lived, which we hope will be of interest.

Putting up the Stiles

Walk - Directions

Directions for the walk will be printed here in italics. The numbers relate to the numbers on the map in the centre of this book or on the leaflet. It is a fairly gentle historic ramble of 11½ miles. Allow about 6 hours. It is easily possible to use any number of public paths which cross the valley to shorten the walk and make a smaller loop.

The start of the walk is based on the public car park by the Swan Inn at Aston Munslow. Alternative parking can be found in the layby at Broncroft or the car parks of the other pubs aldjacent to the route. Please seek the landlords' permission before using these pub car parks. There is limited parking at other points along the route near Bouldon and in Diddlebury.

Walkers are asked to observe the Country Code, to respect the countryside and the people who live in it.

The first Waymarker

A well-deserved pint

The name

Corve is from the Old English word corf, a cutting. The river Corve flows from Bourton to where it joins the Teme on the outskirts of Ludlow. The valley is between the Clee hills to the south east and Wenlock Edge to the north west. Brown Clee, at 540m, is the highest point in Shropshire. From earliest times Corvedale provided an easy route between what are now Wales and England.

The first men

When the last ice cap retreated, around 8000 BC, the land was inhabited by migrating groups of animals, and they would have moved around in search of food and water. Often they would follow the course of a river. The late Palaeolithic and Mesolithic people, Britain's first inhabitants, were gatherers, fishers and hunters. They would have trailed their prey, the animals.

Around 4000 BC the Neolithic people arrived. They grew crops and herded animals, and they had a religion for which they created 'henges' such as Stonehenge, burial mounds and long barrows.

Neolithic and Bronze Age materials, crop marks, and possibly the mound after which Munslow is named, show there was prehistoric life in Corvedale. There may have been a barrow at Thonglands. There was a Bronze Age settlement and tumuli at Bromfield, south west of the walk, where Ludlow race course now is.

Early trade

Trade gradually developed, as people found a need for essentials such as tools and salt. There were special areas where they made stone tools which were traded all over the country. One of these places was at Nuneaton, not far to the east, another at Lan Fawr to the west.

At this period Causeway Camps were constructed. They were a series of banks and ditches, with unrestricted entrances which indicated these camps were not for defence. It is possible they were trading or meeting places.

From about 3000 BC people began to use metal for tools; copper, bronze and then iron. Copper was found in Ireland, North Wales, Cornwall, and possibly Cheshire. Tin came mainly from Cornwall. To make bronze both copper and tin were needed, so transport and trade were necessary to combine them. By 2000 BC Britain had a settled society and many well-used trade routes.

Celts and forts

Celtic migration reached the Severn valley by 700 BC. They built the defensive hill forts, of which South Shropshire has an unusually large number. These forts were permanently inhabited, but there is evidence of individual farmsteads outside as well. Some of these may have been fortified. A good example is at Culmington, where a rectangular enclosure has within it a small circular one, possibly the site of a house.

Also at Culmington is Camp Ring, about which nothing is known. Much of Nordy Bank, on the slopes of Brown Clee Hill, still exists, but the other camps on the Clee Hills have vanished due to the extensive mining and quarrying there. The largest in Shropshire, 28 hectares, used to be on the summit of Titterstone Clee, where the radar domes are. The remains of a stone rampart still exist.

The Romans

Then came the Romans. There was fierce resistance in the west for several decades, but Wales, first attacked in 48 BC, was finally subdued by 80 AD. Military roads were built.

A verified one, Watling Street West, ran north/south through or near Craven Arms, connecting Wroxeter, Hereford and Caerleon. Along this the Romans built forts or overnight 'marching camps'. One of these is on the present A49, at Bromfield, on what was called Old Field.

There may have been another Roman road along Corvedale - from Greensforge in Staffordshire through Bridgnorth, then to Ludlow via Aston Eyre, Monkhopton, south of the Corve from just before Shipton, to Beambridge, where it rejoins the modern road through Munslow and Diddlebury. Parts of it are known locally as Rowe Lane. A few significant remains have been found to support this theory.

Saxons and Mercia

When the Roman Empire disintegrated princes of the Cornovii tribe ruled in Central Wales and the borders. There were many local wars and Saxon mercenaries came, reaching the Severn in the mid C7 (seventh century). Many smaller Welsh princedoms amalgamated. In the mid C7 the kingdom of Mercia under Offa absorbed that of the Cornovii. In 779 Offa drove the King of Powys from Shrewsbury, then named Pengwerne, and in 784-96 Offa built his dyke to designate the boundary between England and Wales.

Mercia itself came under Anglo-Saxon rule until their nominee King died in 886. In the C9 and C10 the area was often invaded by the Danes, who destroyed the Priory at Wenlock in 874. This was re-established in 1080 as a Cluniac Priory.

The evidence of settlement by Saxons comes from many place names, such as the ending ham, as in Corfham; a burial ground behind Sutton Court; and detail in some churches, such as at Diddlebury. There was an unusual number of Saxon churches, probably because the area was wealthy from the high quality wool it produced.

In the C10 the county was mapped into shires when Edward the Elder recovered it from the Danes. The area was ruled from Shrewsbury. At around this period a system of taxation developed, based on the hundreds. These were sub-divisions of the shires.

Geology and industry

Rocks from ten of the twelve accepted geological ages are found in Shropshire. The Romans probably mined for lead nearby. Analysis of roof shingles at Wroxeter indicate these may have been quarried by the Romans at Bouldon. There are numerous small quarries where local building material was found, and until 1300 the area was heavily forested, part of the Royal Long Forest.

From 1235 coal was mined on the Clee Hills. Limestone was also mined there, and from the C16, iron. From the mid C19 quarrying of Clee Hill Dhu (meaning black) stone was, and still is, a major local industry. This was basalt, and after the setts were transported by rail to Cardiff and used for building the docks in 1855, this stone was widely used for road surfaces. The Clee Hills are pockmarked with evidence of bell-pits, spoil heaps, and the railway which took the stone to the main railway line at Ludlow. In its heyday up to two thousand people were employed.

However the main occupation in Corvedale was agricultural, it being one of the most fertile valleys in the area.

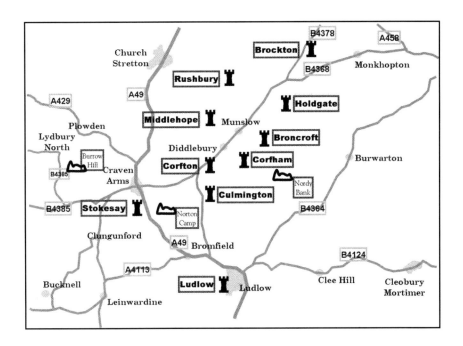

Norman castles

Apart from the Three Castles of the walk there are several castles of Norman origin and even earlier in and near Corvedale. In 1066 there was only one castle in the whole of Shropshire, at Burford. Holdgate, in Corvedale, is mentioned in 1086, Ludlow by 1100, and by 1200 there were around twenty-five castles in the county. Only half a dozen more were built in the C12. By then, of the 186 Norman castles built in England, thirty-two were in Shropshire.

The Norman conquest was aided by their practice of erecting small fortifications along marching routes, and a whole string of defensive forts along the border with Wales, many of them between Offa's Dyke and Watling Street West. At Culmington there is a well-preserved motte and bailey castle, with two other enclosures which were probably extra baileys. Next to it is an example of the medieval ridge and furrow farming system.

Other motte and bailey castles were at Corfton, Holdgate and Brockton, and Middlehope in the next valley, Hopedale. Castles which may have been built later are at Corfham and Broncroft.

The nature of the country, hilly, forested, and in places boggy, made it necessary to use cavalry in these border forts. Fodder and water for horses would be essential, as well as food and water for the garrison. Corvedale was not only a major route through to central Wales, it had good pasture for the horses, and plenty of rivers for water and fish.

Building the castles

If there was no natural site, local labour could be forced to dig a ditch, throwing the earth to the inside to form a mound. This type of castle was already well known in Normandy. A wooden palisade would be built on the top, and a few soldiers left to guard it. The bailey inside the wall was usually rectangular. A higher mound inside, the motte, would have a rough building to give shelter to the garrison commander and his officers, and an observation post for sentries. Building materials often came from demolished houses of the local inhabitants. Huts of wattle and daub, thatched with straw, would shelter the soldiers and their horses and provide necessary storage for grain and essential workmen like blacksmiths.

To begin with, there were probably not enough local sources of food and other essentials. It has been suggested that the Normans, despising trade for themselves, employed Jews, on whom they could depend more than the local population, to organise the supply and transport of these necessities from the rich agricultural lands of the Midlands to the Border forts.

Settling in

Later, when the populace was subdued, there would be time to build or rebuild in stone at the more important sites, and these became administrative centres as well as defensive castles. This is what seems to have happened at Corfham and possibly Broncroft, as well as Holdgate, but many Corvedale castles were less important by this time for defensive uses. Some like Corfton, where no stone building has been found, probably declined. Only in the C13, when there was less need for defence, were fortified manor houses built, such as at Stokesay, and possibly extra building at Broncroft. Instead of being part of the castle community, trades became more separated, moved outside, villages grew up, and fewer people lived in these new manors.

The Welsh and the Borders

Though Wales was first conquered by the Romans, and then the Normans, there were always local Welsh princes stirring up rebellion against the invaders. Welsh border raids usually consisted of brief incursions and rapid withdrawal which tempted the pursuers into following and becoming trapped in difficult and unfamiliar territory.

Captives taken were sold into slavery in Ireland.

The Marcher Lords

William the Conqueror tended to grant lands to his followers in small, scattered pieces, so that they didn't create united mini-kingdoms. However, it was important to have strong defences in the Marches, so a few reliable followers were given concentrated land holdings.

Roger of Montgomery, the first Earl of Shrewsbury, had been one of his main supporters, providing sixty ships for the invasion fleet, and commanding one wing of the army at Hastings. He was given extensive lands in Shropshire and was responsible for defending the central Borders. The Earls of Chester and Hereford guarded to the north and south. By 1086 Earl Roger held over 90% of the lordships and manors in the county, including Culmington and Corfham in Corvedale. Helgot, an undertenant of the Earl, held Millichope, and Roger de Lacy, another undertenant, had Corfton and Stokesay, along with several other manors in the vicinity of Corvedale.

Feudal life

The king granted lands in return for homage, and the lords had to provide money and fighting men and feed the king and his entourage when they were travelling. The lords in turn granted land to vassals with rights and obligations.

Manors might contain several villages, with their open fields, and the peasants had to work for some of the time on the lord's land, and on that of the church. Serfs had few rights. They would be bound to the lord for life, could not own property or marry without permission, but could not be displaced, and did not have to fight. These feudal rulers dispensed justice, minted coins, levied fines and tolls, and demanded military service. When a son inherited he paid homage to his overlord, renewing the vows. If a daughter inherited, the lord arranged her marriage. If there were no heirs, he disposed of the fief (land held in return for feudal service).

However, there were minor rebellions. In 1248, for instance, Herbert of Corfton refused to act as reeve (bailiff or steward) for William Fitz John, Lord of the manor of Heath, although this was one of a bondsman's duties.

Aston Munslow

This village was originally more important than Munslow. In Saxon times it was called Estune - East Town or Farm, indicating that it was to the east of Diddlebury, which was a large parish surrounding Munslow on three sides. In the Domesday survey the pre-Conquest owner of Aston Munslow is named as Almund or Elmund, who also owned the township of Bolledone, or Bouldon, which was part of Culverston Hundred. There was a church, but all traces have vanished. Corn was grown, and there was also a mill.

There were five villagers, eight smallholders, a resident priest, a Frenchman (was he a Norman soldier who had settled or married in the area, or an overseer installed by the Normans?) a rider, or messenger, and six slaves, or serfs. In 1086 it was held by Reginald the Sheriff under Earl Roger of Shrewsbury. It was worth considerably less in 1086 than in 1066, down from 65 to 40 shillings. (One shilling = 5p.) Much of it was 'waste'. The taxable area was 8.5 hides. A hide was the land deemed necessary to feed a household, usually about fifty hectares, though this could vary. It was estimated that in addition to the five ploughs owned a further nine would be possible. This was important to the Normans who needed to provide food for their garrisons. In the C13 the de Hastings family were tenants in chief, holding the manor directly from the King.

There are several houses dating from the sixteenth and seventeenth centuries, some even older. Lower House Farm is late C16, Tudor Cottage early C17.

The Walk begins

Start at the Swan in Aston Munslow from the public car park

The Swan Inn

The car park is actually the village green. The roadside sign 'Dick Turpin slept here' was stolen some years ago - by a C20 highwayman?
    The late C16 Inn was once called the Hundred House, and Justices of the Peace met here. It was first licensed in 1740. The entrance opposite the car park is relatively new, connecting the old Inn and other buildings. There used to be stabling for five horses. All the inns along the roads had stabling.

1   *From the car park, take the lane up the hill to five-ways junction, turn right along the lane.*

2   *Turn right up the next lane (not made up) and go left over the stile just after the chapel. Follow the clearly defined footpath straight ahead over numerous stiles.*

A small Wesleyan Chapel, still used, is on this track just before the field path starts.

If you divert slightly and go straight on for a while at the five-way crossroads, the White House is on the left.

The White House

This was probably the Manor House in medieval times. C13 origins have been found, an undercroft above which a C14 cruck hall was built adjacent to an earlier manor house. At the west end of the hall a timber-framed Tudor wing was built towards the end of the C16, and shortly afterwards the walls were encased in stone.

Between 1780 and 1800 yet another westward extension was built, it is thought possibly after a fire. Earlier rooms, part of the Tudor wing mentioned in an inventory of 1677, may have been destroyed at this time. A new stuccoed front was built across both the new and the Tudor wing.

Outside there is a Norman dovecote. Only lords holding land directly from the King were permitted to build these. The stables remain, as does a cider house. In medieval times the stable was probably a second house, built for other members of the family.

The Purser family moved to the White House in 1947, and Miss Constance Purser turned the house into a Museum of Buildings and Country Life from 1966-86.

She then gave the house to the Landmark Trust, which cares for old buildings and lets them out for holidays. There are still small displays of the Museum's contents in the dairy and kitchen, outhouses, stables and cider house. IT IS NOT OPEN TO THE PUBLIC except when the Landmark Trust holds occasional open days.

The Stedmans

The Stedman family lived at the White House from the C14 until 1946, having risen from yeoman status to that of minor gentry during the C16, making several marriages with the local aristocracy. They are also found at Munslow and Corfton, and the family provided several Rectors.

One of the best known Stedmans was Rowland, who was born at Corfton around 1630 and went on to become an Oxford MA, then Rector of various parishes in the south east. In 1662 he was ejected for non-conformity, but found refuge at Wooburn, Bucks, with the fourth Lord Wharton. He died in 1673, having published some religious books.

Geology of the first part of the path

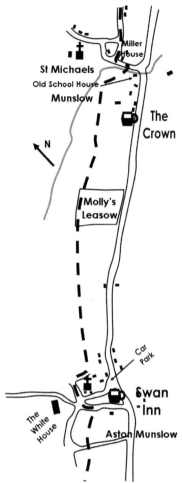

The path here runs along the lower dip slope of the Corvedale Edge half of the Wenlock Edge formation. It passes several small quarries where the underlying rock strata can easily be inspected. These are the youngest beds of the Silurian geological age and part of the Upper Ludlow Shales, which consist of 'thick beds of limestones in association with relatively soft calcareous flags and silt stones'. What you can see is grey-buff coloured crumbly rock in beds of various thicknesses lying approximately parallel to the surface of the ground. This rock is made up of silt and fine sand grains which, when quarried, produce a rather soft building stone. This Munslow Mudstone can be seen in almost all of the older buildings nearby. However, some beds, harder and darker in colour, are associated with the Ludlow Bone Beds which are famous for their fossil shells.

The soils above this rock formation have been derived from it and therefore are of silt plus fine sand and only a little clay content. These are classified here by pedologists as 'acid-brown soils'. Rainfall over the millennia has made them moderately acid but their colour is a greyish brown to a paler grey when really dry.

Field names

Old maps give these, and while some are fanciful most are severely practical. On the path from Aston Munslow to Munslow there are First, Second, Third and Fourth Plough Fields. Then Green Thorns and Molly's

Leasow. Leasow means pasture. Then come Upper Skelding and Piece next Skelding, (though there was a field named Townsend in between.) Elsewhere there are names indicating their use such as Cow Pasture, Ox Leasow, Stallion Meadow and Buck Field, and descriptive ones such as Crooked Acre, Garden Piece, Piece by the Lane, Well Field, Clay Fields, and Church Furlong. Long Furlong usually describes what was once a part of the medieval open field system.

The Apostles' Way and Shropshire Holy Wells

In medieval times the road from Much Wenlock Abbey to St Lawrence's shrine at Ludlow was known as the Pilgrim's Road.

From the mid C17 until the C19 the main road below this part of the path, the B4368, was known as The Apostles' Way, and before the C19 there was an annual procession along it from Munslow to the Aston boundary. Banners, including the 'great banner' of the Crucifixion and of St Michael, were carried, and fixed to the fence of Aston Leasow. A well beside the road in Molly's Leasow, midway between Aston Munslow and Munslow, was dressed and the procession paused to eat and drink.

There were many other holy wells in Shropshire, often associated with some saint. To the west of Aston was the Red Well (or Wall), so named because of the colour of the soil. In the mid C18 the cured hung crutches nearby. Red Wall field is on the road to Middlehope.

3   Cross the stile on your left, to other side of hedge, and continue in same direction with hedge on your right. After next stile, bear right to waymarker post, then half right, down hill to stile, down steps and across bridge to road.

Munslow

The name comes from 'Hlaw', a burial mound or tumulus, but the meaning of 'muns' or 'munsel' is unknown. It might be a man's name. Neolithic and Bronze Age materials have been found, as well as crop marks, showing prehistoric activity in the area.

The village is first mentioned in the C12, and could have been part of Aston Munslow for the purposes of Domesday. The church was moved to Munslow soon after, for in 1115 there was a Rector of Munslow who quarrelled with the Monks of Wenlock over the tithes of

Millichope. This was settled at a judicial hearing in Holdgate Castle. Munslow gradually became more important than Aston Munslow.

The early overlords were the Banestre family, who owned important lands in Cheshire, but at the end of the C12 the overlordship passed to William de Hastings, who was married to one of the Banestre heiresses. The de Hastings later became Earls of Pembroke. In the early C15 the Manor and Rector passed to the Burleys of Broncroft, and later to, amongst others, the Littletons.`

A William de Hastings was known to be tenant at Aston Munslow, and the family held the patronage of Munslow church until 1410, when the Burleys of Broncroft took it over until 1471.

The village contains many C16, C17 and C18 houses, some of which can be seen concentrated around the bend in the main road. The early ones were mainly box framed, but by the C18 most were built of stone. Brick was used occasionally, such as the C17 wing of Munslow Farm, and part of the Crown.

Divert briefly down to the main road for a better view.

The Old School

The Old School House on the corner of the main road was built in 1658 for John Baldwyn and his wife Abigail.

In 1573 the Rector, Roger Stedman, kept a school, and there were dame schools in the parish during the C18.

A school was in this house, which was then named Munslow Old Farm House, around 1840.

A few years later in 1849 the house became a National school, and there were up to ninety pupils in the 1890s. It was financed by voluntary contributions, a small endowment, and school pence paid by the parents. In 1870 there was an adult evening school too. In 1895 only eleven of the school's children lived in the village, the other seventy-six had to walk between one and two and a half miles.

The room where the Infants were taught has a gallery all round. There were rumours of an underground passage linking to a nearby farm, but despite a search by the children nothing was discovered. By 1922 there were fifty-five pupils, and when the school closed in 1982, only twenty-nine. It is now a private residence.

The Baldwyn or Baldwin Family

John Bawderwyn's is the earliest name recorded. The spelling of names changes frequently over the centuries! Henry I granted Mongomery to Baldwin of Bollers. The Welsh name for Montgomery is still Trefaldwyn, Baldwin's town.

An ancestor came over with the Conqueror, and was related to him by marriage. One of them settled in Corvedale in the time of Henry II. A William Baldwin was Cupbearer to Queen Mary Tudor. When he died without a son his brother Roger succeeded him, and he built the moated stone manor of Elsich in about 1545.

Roger married a lady whose family owned Stokesay Castle, and spent many years as an agent of the Earl of Shrewsbury, who had the job of guarding Mary Queen of Scots. He was imprisoned in the Tower of London for three years, and carved his name on the wall of the Beauchamp Tower. He adopted as the family motto *Per deum meum transilio murum* (By the help of my God I shall leap over the wall.)

During the Civil War Sir Charles Baldwin was a Royalist, and was later heavily fined. The family had a long lease on Stokesay Castle and they held it for the King. Sir Charles had represented Ludlow in the Long Parliament, and three other Baldwins were also MPs.

His son Sir Samuel was a barrister and one of the King's sergeants. He was buried in the Temple church. He was great-grandfather of another Charles, MP for Shropshire, whose son William married a Childe heiress and assumed their name.

Other notable Baldwins were Richard, 1616-89, his nephew Richard, and grandson Edward, all physicians who practised in the area. Several members of the family served on Ludlow Corporation. In 1724 a John Baldwin was an attorney in Ludlow. The Munslow Baldwins were descended from a cousin of the Richard who was buried in Diddlebury in 1585, and was the tenth generation from the first John.

In 1752 the family sold Delbury Hall estate in Diddlebury and moved to Worcestershire. The Thomas Baldwin of this time was great-grandfather of Stanley Baldwin, Prime Minister. The family were described as ironfounders, and could have been involved in the many small ironworks around the Clee Hills.

The Crown Inn

A little further back along the main road is the second Inn on the route, the Crown Country Inn, formerly known as the Munslow Inn.

The main part dates from the mid C18, though there are traces of earlier timber-framed building works at the rear. It was licenced in 1790. Before these inns were built alesellers were licenced at both Munslow and Aston Munslow in the C17. The Crown was another of the Hundred Houses where JPs sat.

Legal system of Hundreds

The Anglo-Saxons developed a legal system based on shires, which was effectively the system of government. The shires were divided into hundreds, which were roughly a hundred hides, and these into vills, which became the parishes. In 1086 there were fifteen hundreds in Shropshire, though some areas of the county came under hundreds in neighbouring counties. Many Anglo-Saxon names of hundreds were derived from the tops of hills, tumuli (Munslow) or isolated stones (Culverstone).

Under the Normans the Sheriff governed the county, and had deputies, reeves. Their job was to keep the peace and collect taxes. The county court met two or three times a year to deal with the more important cases. The hundred courts met monthly, presided over by a bailiff, and the judges were some of the more important freemen. Every freeman had to be a member of a tithing, a group of ten men and a leader, and they were responsible for one another's misdeeds.

At the time of Domesday Corvedale had a rather confused system of hundreds, the most complicated in Shropshire, with some parts

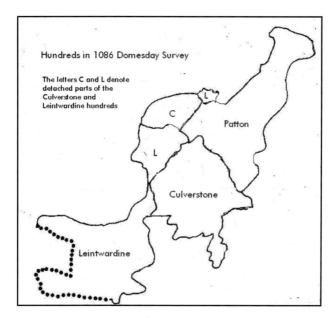

Hundreds in 1086 Domesday Survey

The letters C and L denote detached parts of the Culverstone and Leintwardine hundreds

L

C

Patton

L

Culverstone

Leintwardine

detached from the main area.

Reorganisation did little to simplify it. From the C12 to C14 part of the north-east of what became Munslow parish was under the jurisdiction of Wenlock Priory. Broadstone, further along the B4368 towards Much Wenlock, had been in Rushbury parish in 1086, soon afterwards became owned by Shrewsbury Abbey, and at some time before 1589, possibly after the Dissolution of the Abbeys, was in Munslow parish.

Patton and Culverstone Hundreds were originally paired and had a joint caput, or head, at Corfham, but the meeting place was transferred to Munslow, probably at the end of the C11 or early in the C12. This was more convenient, being on the main road between Ludlow and Much Wenlock.

The new Munslow hundred was formed in the reign of Henry I, combining Patton and Culverstone, but a large portion was removed under Richard I to give to a new liberty (area over which they had jurisdiction) for Wenlock Priory.

The Normans centralised the system of justice, taking more power for the Crown. The custom of appointing local dignitaries as Justices of the Peace began in the late C12, though this title did not come into use until the mid C14. JPs had to live in the county, and own property. They were unpaid apart from minor expenses. They held sittings around the locality, for example in the Corvedale inns, the Crown and the Swan.

Apart from dealing with criminal activities and disputes, by the end of the C16 JPs had acquired many administrative functions, such as maintaining the roads, regulating wages, and administering the Poor

Law. There was an almshouse in Munslow mentioned in 1716, given by a former Minister. It probably lasted until the mid C19, but was gone by the 1880s.

Some other old buildings in Munslow

Munslow Farm, which can be seen on the far side of the main road, has a C17 red brick wing, and an C18 one of coursed stone rubble. The Dean Brook beside it is one of many streams draining into the Corve.

The cottages today

Next to it is The Chains, another farmhouse with C16 origins. It's sale was recorded in 1607. The houses beyond used to be the Bakery and Post Office, both now converted to private houses, and then comes the C17 Glebe Farm, which was once owned by the Church Commissioners.

On the near side of the road is a row of terrace cottages, much altered. The first two used to be a butcher's shop with slaughterhouse and stabling. An old picture shows a shop window in the middle of the terrace, and what looks like a barn with a cart entrance beyond, between it and the last house.

As they used to be

4   Turn left up road and bear right by the horse trough up part tarmac drive/path, then along narrower path to emerge on lane. Continue, bearing slightly right, to Severn Trent Water plant at end of lane; turn right through gate and follow footpath down to cross stile to road.

The Miller House

This house, built on a cliff, is reputed to be on the site of a former Manor belonging to the Littletons, which was partly burnt down in the C16. It was rebuilt in stone around 1799.

You can make a short detour by continuing up the hill and turning left at the first junction to the church, St. Michael's.

St Michael's Church

The nave is C12, the tower late C12 with a C15 top stage and C18 parapet. The chancel is probably C13, and the north aisle C14. There are some medieval features, including a C14 cruck-built south porch with a carving of a dog at the base of the inner cruck on the east side. The  chancel and south nave wall are C13 with later C13 and C14 windows. Some of the bench ends are medieval. There is some good (restored) medieval glass, and an unusual Victorian east window by Evans of Shrewsbury, who also restored the old glass. The Churchman and Baldwyn monuments in the north aisle contain unusual mystical symbols. The old Lych Gate was moved in the C19 to a spot opposite the small door, over the tomb of a former Rector, F. W. Read, who died in 1774.

The church was in decay by the late C18, some repairs were done in 1815 and 1841, and it was heavily restored in 1869-70. What had been the Aston Aisle became the vestry.

The Registers, mostly complete, date from 1538.

The former Rectory, built in the early C19, is beyond the church.

Early Munslow Rectors provided some excitement. Apart from those who were excluded for various reasons, one was murdered in 1298, another excommunicated in 1333, and in 1422 one resigned after being castrated.

Munslow Common

This is to the north west, high on the hill above the church. It was known as Little London when squatters developed a hamlet there, and was enclosed in 1847.

It was a place of recreation. In 1606 there was bearbaiting and in the 1820s hunting. When the rest was enclosed four acres of it were designated Munslow Recreation Ground.

Go back to the junction and carry on up the road to the left until the track joins it at a sharp left bend, and you rejoin the walk route.

Millichope

As you pass the Severn Trent plant Millichope Park is to the left. Though not on the Three Castles Route it is well worth a visit during February weekends to follow the snowdrop trail.

In the C16, when Upper Millichope ceased to be a fief of Wenlock Priory it passed to the Carrington family, who then owned the Aston Hall estate.

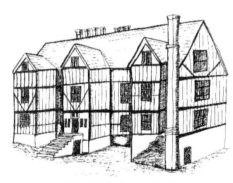

Old Millichope Hall

There was once a large Elizabethan house, which was demolished in 1843, on a lower level than the present one. The new house was built in 1835-40, and remodelled in the C20.

The park was landscaped in the C18, with an Ionic Rotunda facing the house across a lake. This consisted of three pools in 1817 and was enlarged in the mid C19, fed by waterfalls. There was an obelisk and a deer park.

During WWII, between 1943-5, a Roman Catholic girls' school run by Augustinian nuns was evacuated from Westgate on Sea to Millichope Hall. Afterwards Benedictines from Prinknash Abbey lived there until 1947. Between 1948-62 the Hall was used as a boys' boarding school.

In 1772 the Lordship of the Manor, with the Manor House, but no other local property, was sold to Robert, Lord Clive, and his descendants sold it in 1842 to the Revd. R. N. Pemberton of Millichope Park. The Clive family owned other properties in the Ludlow area.

The Littleton family

There were several branches of the Littleton or Lyttleton family in Shropshire and the West Midlands, and to complicate the genealogy they intermarried. They owned Broncroft Castle in the C15, but later exchanged it for Millichope Park. Earlier they lived at Munslow Farm.

Edward Littleton was born at Munslow in 1589 and became a noted lawyer, serving from 1621 as Chief Justice of North Wales. He was also MP for Leominster and closely involved in the Parliamentary sessions of the 1620s. He became Recorder of London and in 1641 was given the title Lord Littleton of Munslow. At the start of the Civil War in 1642 he sent the Great Seal to the King at York. He raised a Royalist regiment of foot, and became their Colonel. He died in 1645.

Deer parks

At Millichope and elsewhere parks were created and enclosed for hunting. In Domesday there were thirty-six lays in the county, enclosures for breeding deer before releasing them for hunting. At Corfton one is described as for 'catching roe deer'. In 1281, twenty-four roe deer were sent from Hampshire to stock the Long Forest.

Deer hunting in late Saxon times was the preserve of the Crown and aristocracy. Under the Normans this Crown prerogative was extended by the imposition of forest laws.

The Forester's Lodge at Upper Millichope

This dates from the C12 and was the house of the King's Forester in the Long Forest. It is probably the oldest domestic building in Shropshire. There are three storeys, each a single room. Extremely thick walls and the original entrance in the upper storey were for protection. Foresters were not popular officials. It is now part of a farmhouse.

There may once have been a mill here - the name is suggestive.

The Long Forest

This extended from near Craven Arms to Buildwas, and north to Lyth Hill. It contained lots of oak trees. Forests were not always dense thickets, many had open spaces, and they were the favourite hunting grounds of kings. It is probable that in Henry II's reign Clee Forest became a private chase. Other forests were the Wyre, Brewood, and Mount Gilbert round the Wrekin. Both the latter and the Long Forest were changing, becoming partially cultivated, by 1086.

Under Henry III more woodland resources were taken for the use of the crown or granted to others. The forests were used for timber, charcoal, oak bark for tanning, honey and beeswax for candles.

Woodland was being cleared in the C13 and more intensive agriculture practised on heaths, moors, and poorer land. Wenlock Priory cleared a lot of Clee Forest in the late 1290s and a major reduction of forests was forced on the Crown. Little was left in the county apart from the King's demesne woods (those reserved for his profit or enjoyment).

Around 1300 Aston Munslow, Munslow, Millichope and other parts of Corvedale were declared disforested.

Lower Millichope

When a youth club was started, a disused cowshed near Beambridge belonging to the Millichope Estate was converted, and later became the Village Hall.

5   *Take care crossing busy road. Over stile opposite and continue ahead (may be muddy in winter). Bear right at waymarker before white cottage, through gate onto lane; turn left and alongside river (Corve).*

Turnpikes

These were toll roads built by private investors where barriers (swinging bars - thus turnpike) or gates blocked the roads to force travellers to stop and pay fees.

This main road between Much Wenlock and Ludlow, with a branch to Craven Arms, was a turnpike between 1756-1867. The first house on the left looking towards Munslow village used to be the toll house. It is still called the Gatehouse. There was another toll house at Beambridge to the east.

The road west of Bouldon was turnpiked between 1784 and 1873.

Inns

As well as the three Inns close to the route along the B4368, there is also the Seven Stars past Hungerford, which had a full licence in 1840. In 1889 the landlord of the Seven Stars was fined for opening during prohibited hours, and the landlord of the Swan for permitting drunkenness.

There were other inns along the road or nearby, the Buck's Head at Hungerford, and the Butcher's Arms at Primrose Bank, Thonglands, which was open 1851-1920. An aleseller was licensed here in the C17, as they were in most other villages.

Agriculture

In 1086 about 22% of Shropshire land was arable, compared with 50% in the Midlands and East Anglia. By the C13 most villages seemed to have strips in the open field system. Some traces remain in the village of Burley, west of Culmington.

There were cottage gardens to grow vegetables, flax and hemp, and the peasants could sell the surplus for cash, which was needed to pay various dues. By 1300 there were no great expanses of open fields or large villages, but many small villages, woods, moors, and pastures on the uplands. In the mid C12 fishponds were constructed, stocked with trout and pike.

Ploughing was done by oxen. In the mid C13 Corfton manor was restocked with oxen. Horses were rarely used for ploughing, but were for harrowing and portering.

Before 1274 the Templars at Holdgate sent some oats to Ludlow, and were ambushed by men described as the bailiff of the Lord of Corfham. They stole the grain, sowed it and harrowed it with the horses they had also taken.

Cattle and sheep have always been here in Corvedale. Sheep, over the years, have become more important. By the C18 sheep in the southern part of the Dale were often grazed on Brown Clee. They were the most common animal, but there were also pigs, goats and poultry. There was a dovecote at Holdgate in the late C13.

After 1750 there were general improvements with machinery, but this helped create much rural poverty. In the 1790s, for example, no Munslow labourer's family kept a pig or brewed beer or bought butcher's meat. Some might have cheese, but in a large family all of a man's wages were needed for wheat or flour. Many needed parish help. Labourers' cottages were often very poor, only mud huts.

The 'great depression' after 1870, when cheap grain imports drove prices down, stimulated an increase in mixed farming, and Corvedale farming was prosperous.

Enclosures

Much of early Corvedale agriculture was by the medieval strip farming system in three (usually) big open fields with crop rotation.

For convenience, probably due to the nature of the land, there were many early and agreed enclosures between the early C16 and the mid C18. There had been enclosures on Brown Clee since the C15.

The forced enclosures of later centuries which caused such distress elsewhere affected Corevedale only marginally.

Timber sales went with clearances, such as the Earl of Shrewsbury's wood at Diddlebury and William Savage's Corfton Wood in 1575.

On the enclosed estates some of the common land was whittled away. For example, in 1732 there were fourteen squatters who had erected huts on Hayton's Bent, and on the Clee Hills miners built squatters' cottages on the commons.

Brook House

The bridge across the Corve is by Brook House, known as Brook Hall as early as 1589.

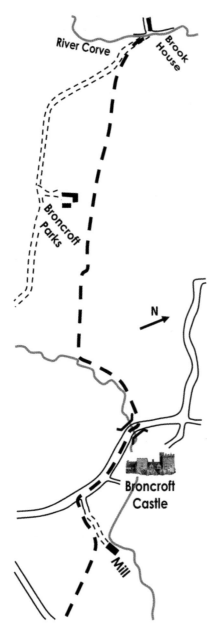

6 *Cross bridge, bear right over stile, across field, then left along line of hedgerow over several stiles (past Broncroft Parks on your right) until you reach the river.*

Broncroft Parks

On the right is Broncroft Parks, once the deer park of the Castle. In 1334 a grant was made to Hugh Tyrell and his heirs for ever 'of free warren in demesne lands in Broncroft'. Only Lords of the Manor were permitted to rear rabbits, which had been brought to England by the Normans.

The Broncroft Parks' farmhouse was kept by the Littletons after they moved from Broncroft to Munslow. The C17 farm house is the last remaining house of a small settlement, and is timber-framed beneath the rendering added by the Church Commissioners after WWII.

Geology in the valley

The route from here is almost all underlain by the rock formations belonging to the Upper Old Red Sandstone geological age. Quarries are rare, so the rock is best seen at Broncroft Castle, where it is a coarsely grained medium-red sandstone. Elsewhere the deep alluvial deposits and red clay ridges cover it up.

7 Cross stile on your left before river, follow river bank over three more stiles to lane.

8 Turn right along lane past Broncroft Castle (NO PUBLIC ACCESS).

Broncroft Castle

It was formerly spelt Bromcroft, meaning a broomy croft or enclosure.

In 1086 Broncroft was a bereweek (a detached piece of farmland of the manor reserved for the lord's own use) of Corfham. The dovecote dates from Norman times. The Burley family acquired it from the Tyrells in about 1361. The stone castle building was reputedly begun by Sir Simon Burley in 1382 on the site of Saxon and Norman remains. Sir Simon was a sailor, soldier, and ambassador. He served in the army under Edward III's son, the Black Prince, and was tutor to the Prince's son, later Richard II. He was executed in 1386.

The rest of the castle was built soon afterwards. It was a fortified house of similar plan to Stokesay, two strong towers connected by a Hall. The only remains of the medieval building are the lower parts of the towers to the right of the entrance.

After 1450 the castle belonged to several different people, including members of the Burley and Littleton families. The Lutley family held it from the early C17 until 1805.

The Burleys

William, Sir Simon's great-great-nephew, was, from around 1436, an MP in eighteen parliaments and twice Speaker of the House of Commons, in 1436 and 44.

His father John was High Sheriff of Shropshire, as was William.

Civil War skirmishes

No major battles have taken place in Corvedale, but there were local skirmishes, as well as incursions by the Welsh.

In 1642, during the Civil Wars, Broncroft was garrisoned for the King by Adam Lutley.

In June 1645 the retreating royal forces abandoned and dismantled the fortifications, attempting to make it unusable.

Cromwell's troops, approaching Ludlow, took it, and recognising how important it was for protecting the road to Ludlow 'fell to repair and fortify' it. Lord Calvine was appointed Governor.

The Parliamentarians were defeated in a further skirmish on July 4th when many were killed and wounded. The Royalists, with between three and four hundred men, won, taking fifty prisoners and eighty 'good horses', but the Parliamentarians continued to garrison the castle.

Four Parliamentary troopers were buried at Munslow between July 3rd and August 4th that year, but how they died is uncertain.

Broncroft was not demolished because it was not considered big enough to be a threat. However, in 1648 on July 11th Parliament gave orders to make it untenable. The towers were the only parts not entirely destroyed.

The Castle restored

Most of the present building is mid C19. It was rebuilt and made habitable by the Johnstone family in the second quarter of the C19, and extended in the 1890s. Broncroft has changed hands several times in the C20.

9   Immediately beyond drive by pair of cottages, go over stile on left
     and continue parallel to drive to corner of field, turn right along field
     boundary, over stile on left, and around boundary of next field to
     stile at top left hand corner of field, to road.

Broncroft Mill

There has probably been a mill on this site since medieval times,
although the earliest documentary reference to the present mill is in
1770.

Shropshire mills

In Domesday ninety-eight mills were recorded in the county and there
were more by the C13. They were mostly water rather than horse-
driven, and many had fish ponds, and eel and fish traps.
    There were just a couple of windmills mentioned in 1267, at
Shrewsbury and Wem, and only two more by the C14. There were
probably others later, if the name Windmill Field, west of Aston

Munslow, is an accurate description.

Fulling mills for scouring and thickening cloth were established in Ludlow and elsewhere in the late C12, because of the importance of wool for export.

10 *Cross road, go over stile, continue up field edge, through gate and into wood. At waymarker post bear half right onto permissive track, follow this and at area where new plantings begin, bear right on main track down to road.*

Diversion - Holdgate

Holdgate parish is of interest because part of it is now in Munslow, Bouldon once belonged to it, and it was a more important administrative centre than Corfham, several court cases having been heard there. Some early masonry remains.

There is no evidence of prehistoric or Roman settlement. The parish was probably formed in the C11. Before 1066 it was part of an estate called Stantune. A castle, Helgot's Castle, named after the man William the Conqueror gave it to, was built before 1086, and gave the village its name. In the C12 Henry I was entertained here. The castle was rebuilt in stone about 1280.

In 1244 Richard, Earl of Cornwall, became the Lord, but the Templars leased it from him between 1263 and 1284. They had several properties in Shropshire after 1158, especially in Corvedale, including Lawton Mill near Diddlebury, but their main Priory was at Stanton Long.

The castle motte survives, and a free-standing tower house with huge corner turrets was built in the bailey around the end of the C13. In 1292 the old castle was said to be worth nothing, and in 1383 was in ruins. Parts of the castle (perhaps the tower house) remained until the castle was besieged and pulled down by Royalists in 1644. In 1648 Parliament sold it. A brick tower was mentioned at this time. The surviving part is now incorporated into a farmhouse.

There was a church, which seems to have been part of the castle, and a priest in 1086. A secular college was there from before 1210 until about 1373. There was a water mill by the early C13, but it was not mentioned after 1346.

A weekly market was established in 1222. Holdgate paid a fee of five marks and a palfrey (a lady's saddle horse). In 1284 it had toll income of 6s 8d. These markets sold staple goods and animals. Bigger

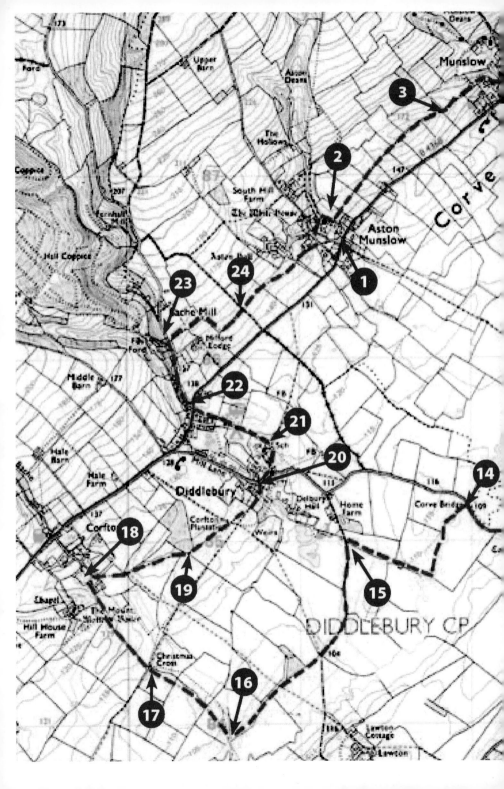

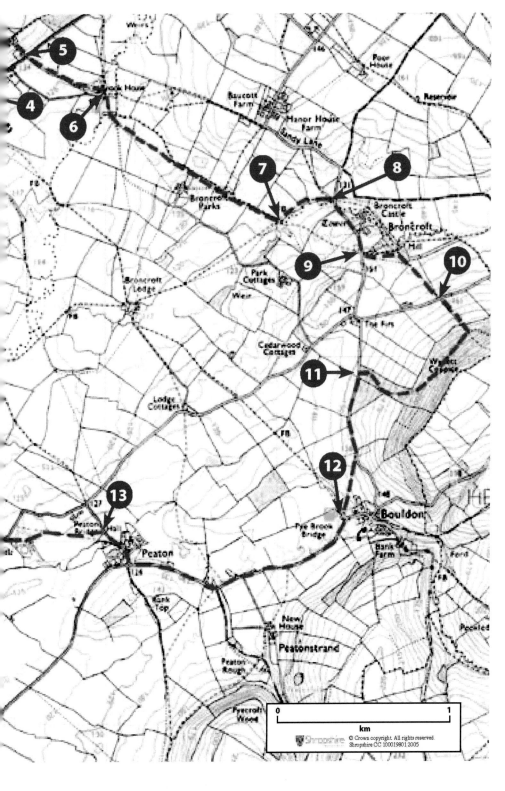

markets in towns also sold cloth and wine. Markets were established later by Royal Charter.

Holdgate had another market and fair in 1291, but both seem to have lapsed soon afterwards. Fairs drew merchants from a wider area, often once a year, for two to five days.

The road from Bridgnorth comes through Holdgate to Broncroft, and by the C13 led from there to Corfham, Diddlebury and Ludlow.

By 1255 Holdgate barony had its own court, which met twice a year. It was still meeting in the 1590s and a variety of courts met until the C19.

11 *Turn left along road for approx. 700 yards. Just beyond gates on either side of road, go over stile on right, then diagonally left across field to stile in corner (by Tally Ho Inn, white building).*

Geology between Broncroft and Peaton

The soil is remarkably uniform in its browny-red colour. The clay content varies, however, and is sufficiently high to really stick to boots, especially around Peaton.

Bouldon

This is slightly off the route, where the Clee or Pye Brook drains towards the Corve. In 1086 it was Bolledone, in 1166 Bullandon. The 'dun' means hill, and 'bula' means bullock. Bouldon was subject to the Holdgate barony court, and even in 1863 this court appointed the Bouldon constable. From 1595 the Baldwins owned the manor.

Until the late C11 the village was part of Diddlebury, then it became a detached portion of Holdgate parish. It was transferred to Diddlebury in 1881 for civil purposes and in 1926 for ecclesiastical.

Most of the houses are C16 or C17. The cedar wood houses at Bouldon, Peaton Strand and Peaton were erected in the 1950s by the Church Commissioners, who purchased the Holder estate in 1942. The main house is Bouldon Farm.

The open fields had mostly been enclosed by 1733. A water mill was mentioned in 1611, described as a runcorn (mixed grains) mill in 1733. It was probably the mill which was on a leet from Pye brook at the east of the village, and working until 1934. Another water mill, probably to the west, near Old Mill Meadow, was mentioned in 1570, but was gone by 1842.

There were iron furnaces in the C17, and field names Furnace Wood and Furnace Field recall this. In 1643 a 'clerk of the furnace' made sixty-three tons of ordnance for the King, delivered from Bouldon to Shrewsbury and Bridgnorth, and a similar amount in 1644, including a gun to defend Ludlow. There was cordwood from Ditton Priors, ironstone from Brown Clee, and limestone from Bouldon. In the C17 and C18 the village contained the ironworks of the Blount family. In 1717 the works recorded an output of four hundred tons per year.

By the C18 pig iron was the main product, and reputed to be the finest in England. Later this mill probably became the paper mill. Paper was being made here by 1803, until 1851. Another product was sandstone flags, and limestone and building stone were also quarried until 1850. From analysis of stone at Wroxeter it has been suggested the Romans quarried Bouldon slabs.

A chapel existed in 1737, probably at Bouldon Farm where burials were found in 1800 in the garden and under the house. In 1873 a small iron chapel, All Saints, opened, built at the Rector of Holdgate's expense, but it was closed by the 1980s and later demolished.

BOULDON CHURCH

12 Forward across car park in front of Tally Ho, turn right along road 1 mile to Peaton. At Peaton, turn right on road, through farm complex and across river bridge.

Peaton Strand

At Peaton Strand to the right of the road are the remains of the lower parts of a Primitive Methodist chapel, in use between 1873 and 1984. The adjoining Chapel Cottage was the minister's house.

Non-conformism in Corvedale

In the C17 and early C18 several families were Catholics, including the Smiths, who were Lords of Aston Manor, and the Wrights and Blounts of Bouldon.

Methodists met at Aston Munslow in 1804, and a house in the parish was licenced for worship in 1827. The Wesleyan Chapel in Aston was built in 1862. In 1804 a room in a Holdgate farm was licenced for Methodist use, and Primitive Methodists preached at Bouldon from 1828, in a house belonging to John Jones.

There were other Methodist Chapels at Primrose Bank (1861-1963) and a Wesleyan one at Bache Mill (1879 -1964). This one, now a house, is further along the route.

Other chapels

There was a chapel at Broadstone, on the B4368, but nothing remains. For a time services were held twice a year, on Christmas Day and Good Friday, in a barn.

The best-preserved and earliest chapel in the area is the Norman Chapel in a field at Heath, which is a deserted village on the lower slopes of Brown Clee, a mile east of Bouldon.

The chapel, built in 1090 and relatively unchanged since, has a C19 window. On the nave wall are traces of a painting of George and the Dragon. There is a C17 pulpit, reader's desk, squire's pew, box pews and altar rails.

Heath Chapel

Peaton

This is an Anglo-Saxon place name, the tun or settlement of Peatta. As late as 1306 the village was burnt by a Welsh raiding party.

Peaton Lodge, in trees to the right on the corner, is a C17 building refronted in the late C18 in a style common to many Corvedale farms, with elliptical-headed casement windows. Opposite are cedar wood houses which were built by the Church Commissioners.

Peaton Hall Farm

Peaton Hall Farm further on to the right is a large C17 timber-framed but stone-faced building. It belonged to Mr Atherden, who altered it greatly in the early C20. He was a retired Ludlow banker.

The stone cottages in the lane, past the cedar wood houses, were designed by the Powis Castle estate office for him.

Midland Counties Dairies had a milk collection point at Peaton, and milk in ten-gallon churns was taken to Cadbury's at Marlbrook, near Leominster. During the mid-war period milk production in Corvedale increased a great deal.

In the 1930s Percy Giles Holder, who had acquired most of the estates in the area, established one of the largest dairy firms in England at Peaton Hall Farm, but the herd was wiped out by brucellosis. A herd of pigs suffered swine fever twice and was wiped out, then in the winter of 1939/40 a thousand sheep were frozen solid during the lambing season. Mr Holder sold out and Peaton Farm was empty by the time the factory moved in.

Cedar wood houses

Wartime factory

The cattle sheds on the opposite side of the road to Peaton Hall Farm were requisitioned in WWII for a factory between 1940-44, and camouflaged. Fuel tanks for Stirling bombers were made here. At the entrance is a small sentry house and behind it a weigh bridge.

At the far side of the field beyond the bridge over the Pye Brook were the piggeries and another sentry house.

This factory was set up by a Birmingham company, Hurry Heaters, who had made domestic boilers before they moved to Peaton. After the war they returned to Birmingham and Droitwich, making domestic and industrial water heaters.

Both local men and women, and skilled sheet metal workers from Birmingham, were employed. Some cycled to work, others were brought in by a dozen or more busses from Ludlow. Many had to walk miles to be picked up on the way by the busses.

The sheds were heated by large iron stoves, on which bread could be toasted. Tea was brought round morning and afternoon.

Men did the rivetting, the women stamped out the metal shapes or cleaned the tanks with old rags. The Brummies were billeted in the area and went home every third

The Piggeries

weekend. Local lads would sell them rabbits and pigeons at the gate as they left.

Electricity was brought up the Dale for the factory, but no one else had it connected until after the war.

The farm house was turned into offices, and the Company Secretary kept a loaded shotgun by his desk, which he used to scare birds from the garden of the house he rented nearby.

The workers played football for charity, men in dresses against women in shorts.

On the left just before the bridge is Brook Cottage, C17 timber-framed.

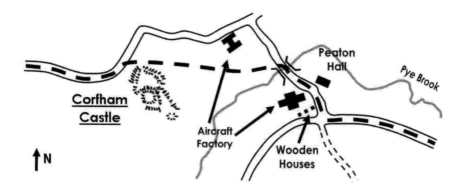

13 Go over stile on your left then across field, no clear line through pasture, keep lone pine to your right and head for group of trees with interpretation board for Corfham Castle on top of small mound.

(Note that the lumps and bumps and the south west corner of the field are the remains of Corfham Castle. Walkers may explore the groundworks of the remains of the castle at their own risk and if they do not disturb either the livestock, which are normally in the field, or the castle ruins.)

To continue from the interpretation board, bear slightly right from the line you were previously walking and go over the stile in the corner of the field and onto the road. Turn left along the road to cross bridge over the River Corve.

Corfham Castle

The probable layout is shown on the Interpretation Board, on the mound outside the moat ditch.

Corfham (land surrounded by the Corve) is the earliest place name in the parish of Diddlebury, dating from early Saxon settlement.

Corfham was a royal manor before the Norman Conquest, and the caput, or head, of Culverston and Patton hundreds. Many hundreds were paired in this way, and it has been suggested that King Edward the Confessor may not have had a royal manor in Patton hundred, so this pairing could have been his way of maintaining a presence there. In Domesday Book it had three ploughs and was worth £6, though it had been worth £10 in 1066.

Many motte and bailey castles erected by the Normans were later abandoned, but sites like Corfham were strengthened with stone keeps and curtain walls. Early castles, following the motte and bailey pattern, tended to have

strong central keeps, often on a mound. In Edward I's time, mid C13, concentric castles were constructed, with several defensive walls with towers rather than a central keep. An archeological survey of the 1970s describes traces of an 'Edwardian' stone castle at Corfham. A few stones can be seen on the raised sections.

Whether there was anything there before the stone castle was built is debatable. Some sources suggest the stone castle was constructed in the early C13. A castle is mentioned in 1233. These traces showed a rectangle measuring 50m east/west, by 46m. Within this is a stone building 30m east/west by 24m. At the north west corner was a round tower, 7m diameter, and suggestions of round towers at the north east and south east corners, with probably a larger rectangular tower at the south west corner. This rectangle was enclosed by a moat. To the north of this inner bailey was an outer one 70m east/west by 50m, enclosed

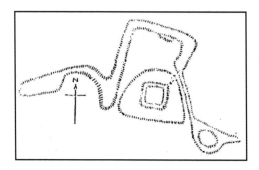

by a much deeper moat. There was also a chapel, first mentioned in 1299, and still used in 1422, and some accounts suggest there was a village, another of those deserted in medieval times.

This double moat was filled by diverting water from Pye Brook 400m to the east north east. At the beginning of the C20 the moat was still filled with water. Old diagrams show a wider section to the west, roughly parallel to the road, the purpose of which is unknown, but as most castles had fish ponds it could have been one. Pye Brook is still a noted trout stream.

The Corfham estate, which then included Culmington and Seifton, was in 1155 given by Henry II to Hugh de Perriers. When he died in 1175 the manor reverted to the King, and it was rated as a royal demesne. Three years later Henry gave the manor to Walter de Clifford, but,

Pye Brook

unusually, he was not named in the Pipe Rolls as the grantee. Walter was the father of Henry's mistress, Fair Rosamund, who had died the previous year, and one of Corfham's towers was referred to as Rosamund's Tower. There used also to be a Rosamund's well in a field below the bridge and on the east bank of the Corve. No trace of it now remains.

If Walter did not possess the manor or whatever castle existed in Henry's time, prior to her death, it is unlikely Rosamund ever visited it. Three fields opposite the castle were called King's Croft.

In the C15 the castle was acquired by the Talbot Earls of

Shrewsbury.

A castle may well have been built here to control the Forest of Clee. Giving this particular manor to the Cliffords could have been because Walter already possessed rights over much of Clee forest, being the Warden.

Fair Rosamund

Walter de Clifford was almost certainly born before 1116, the son of Richard Fitz Ponce, who was recorded in Domesday as holding several manors. They were descended from the Dukes of Normandy.

He took the name Clifford when his marriage brought him Clifford Castle in Herefordshire. His wife Margaret was descended from the Earls of Hereford.

His daughter Rosamund was probably born before 1140. Little is known about her early life, but she may have been educated at Godstow Nunnery near Oxford. Walter owned property in Oxfordshire.

When Rosamund became Henry's mistress is not known. The Rev. Eyton suggests it was around 1154. None of the legends surrounding her name were mentioned until a hundred or more years after her death, and have clouded the facts. Henry openly acknowledged her in 1174/5, and she died soon afterwards and was buried at Godstow.

She may have lived at Woodstock, where there was a royal manor, but the maze or labyrinth protecting her is a C14 legend. The C16 story about Queen Eleanor finding her and offering her poison or a dagger is certainly untrue, since Eleanor had been imprisoned by Henry in 1173 after she encouraged three of their sons to rebel against him, and she remained in prison for most of the rest of Henry's life.

Rosamund was supposed to have borne two sons, but the dates and facts are unclear, and this rumour was not reported until the C17.

One was supposed to be Geoffrey, Archbishop of York, who was born around 1151, when she was only about twelve or fourteen years old. Not impossible, but his mother's name is given as Ykennai.

William Longsword, the other, was supposedly born in 1175, and Henry granted him a manor in Lincolnshire before 1188. Later this manor was claimed by another, different Clifford family from Cumberland, which could explain the confusion.

The later Cliffords

The Cliffords had considerable land holdings in Corvedale. Walter de Clifford had several sons, and on his death around 1190 Corfham passed to the second son, Richard. This was disputed by the eldest son Walter II, and in return for a life annuity Richard gave up Corfham. Walter immediately gave the Canons of Haughmond Abbey mills at Culmington and Seifton.

This Walter was a favourite of King John, was often at Court, and held positions such as Sheriff of Herefordshire. In 1208 he offered a fine of a thousand marks 'not to have an enquiry made as to his behaviour while he was sheriff.' A mark was worth 13s 4d, so this was a vast sum for the time, almost £7,000.

Walter III succeeded about 1220, and was described as a distinguished soldier. In 1233 he was a confederate of Richard, Earl Marshall, who was threatening rebellion. His lands, including Corfham, were seized but soon restored, possibly because his wife Margaret was a daughter of Llewellyn, and the King wanted his support against the Welsh insurgencies. However, in January 1250 'not least amongst the Barons Marchers, in power, wealth, and privileges, he was accused of violent and disgraceful treatment of a King's messenger.' He made the man swallow the King's message, seal and all. He lost his privileges, was fined a thousand marks, and was lucky not to lose his life.

He died in 1263, with only one daughter, Matilda, and since his debts had not all been paid his lands were seized for the Crown. She was a widow, and inherited the Barony, but was abducted by John Giffard of Brimsfield, and their marriage was legalised in 1271.

The Giffards

In 1274 there were many complaints about the behaviour of John Giffard and his officers at Corfham, including releasing felons without trial. After Matilda's death in 1283 he continued to hold the Manor, and when he died in 1299 the whole of it, including Culmington, was worth £20 10s 8d per annum, with the Castle and holdings at Corfham worth little, for the buildings were in a state of collapse. Eleanor, their eldest daughter, inherited Corfham and married Fulke Le Strange of Blakemere. By 1550 only one of the castle towers remained. As with many other ruined castles, it is probable that local people acquired the stone for their own buildings.

Medieval castle life

In early castles the ground floor would have been beaten earth, and the first floor usually wood. The ground floor was for storage and living space for soldiers and servants. The first floor was the Great Hall, where meals were taken, and above that private accommodation for the lord and his family

Diners were often amused by music, jugglers, acrobats or troubadours. Most of these people would travel round the country, dispensing gossip as well as diversions, though the more important lords might employ their own entertainers.

This communal life gradually gave way to more private living, the family dining separately in the solars above the hall.

There was almost always a chapel, usually near the hall for the lord's convenience. Carpets were not used on floors till the C14. Rushes and herbs were spread, swept out and replaced occasionally. There were fireplaces and hearths by the C12, especially when there were first floor halls. By the C14 glazed windows were common.

The kitchen was in the bailey, and in another corner of this there were often fruit trees and vines, plus herb plots. Water came from wells inside the bailey, and sometimes there was a cistern on the roof with pipes to lead the water to some rooms. Latrines, or guardrobes, were normally at the ends of short passages and emptied into the moat.

Medieval villages

The smallest might consist of just a dozen families. Peasants lived in huts with earth floors, no windows or chimneys, and often one end was used for sheltering livestock. This helped keep people warm.

Unlike the lords, their diet was sparse and monotonous, variety depending on what they could grow in their own small patches.

They had some rights, such as collecting dead wood from the forests, pasturing animals on the commons, and collecting nuts. Some villeins (free villagers) were comparatively wealthy. For instance, in 1248 Herbert of Corfton, villein, claimed to have been robbed of eight draught animals, six rams, five wainloads of corn, six bushels of wheat flour and three of oatmeal, four ells of cloth, nine linen sheets and four napkins.

Deserted villages

Aerial photography has given us much information about prehistoric sites, and other places that were once thriving communities. At Heath and near Holdgate, both held by the Barons of Holdgate under the priors of Wenlock, large humps are clearly visible showing where buildings, now overgrown, once were.

Many former villages such as Thonglands are now little more than individual farms, or very much smaller than they used to be. There is an unusual number of these deserted or shrunken villages in and around Corvedale. Within the Dale are Baucott, Broncroft, Corfham and Lawton. On the slopes of the Clee Hills there are remains at Abdon, Cold Weston, and Witchcot. Further into the Clee Hills are Kinson, Egerton and Lower Ingardine. At the last count there were thirty-nine in the area.

Depopulation had a variety of causes. In 1315-19 wet and cold weather destroyed harvests, then came the Black Death in 1348-50, and other outbreaks of plague, agricultural depressions when harvests failed, many animals died, and the villagers left. In 1340 all but two of the tenants at Cold Weston absconded to avoid paying the required taxes. Cattle murrain, or pestilence, was blamed. In 1404 it was claimed that the Welsh sacked a third of the county and people were forced to flee.

Changing land tenure

Towards the end of the middle ages there were changing forms of land tenure, with more leases and outright sales of land, even by peasants. This contrasts with the former system of rents paid in goods, for example hens. Once the Lord of Corfham received eighty-four hens, worth seven shillings (thirty-five new pence), as rent.

Vast changes in land ownership happened after 1540 and the dissolution of the monasteries. Newcomers bought much monastic land. Some older families were breaking up and selling land. Wealthy established gentry, merchants and lawyers, were also purchasing estates.

From the C16 squatters began encroaching on common land by building small huts. Many worked in the Clee Hill mines and quarries.

Initially they were fined 6d a year (2.5p) but after twenty years they were put on the official manorial rent roll.

Landowners often tried to consolidate their holdings as they enclosed land or created parks. At Corfton William Baldwyn and Charles Foxe exchanged land and by the mid C17 most of the township was enclosed. In the 1630s Diddlebury and Seifton were also enclosed. Less was done on the Craven estate and lots of commons were untouched.

In the C18 and C19 ownership of these estates was relatively stable, and before 1914 only a few of the big ones were sold, such as Culmington, but after 1918 many others changed hands.

14 *Go left over stile by waymarker post for permissive path, follow river bank for two fields, then turn right along fence through gate to next field, cross bridge over ditch and continue over stile in corner of field and then left through adjacent gate.*

Wartime, including bombs

On the whole Corvedale escaped bombing, though it was on the flight path as German bombers made for Liverpool. An occasional bomb was dropped, and on one occasion the whole load of bombs fell, either because the pilot had lost his way or because he was in trouble and had to turn back.

15 *Continue ahead along track/field boundary and through two gates, then keep along line of hedge to right (block of marshy woodland other side of hedge), over stile ahead and nearly to corner of next field.*

16 *Turn right over the second of two small bridges, then cross field bearing slightly right, cross double stile then, keeping hedge to right, two more stiles to emerge onto stoned track at bend (Christmas Cross).*

Christmas Cross

The origin of this name is unknown, but there are various theories for other 'Christmas' place names. It could be associated with a family of that name, but there is no evidence here of houses. It could relate to

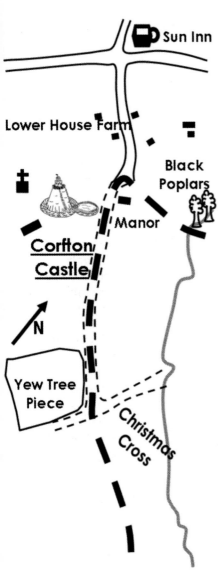

some unusual Christmas event nearby. It could be a place from where people gathered Christmas holly. The field to the north east was known as Yewtree Piece, and yews are associated with Christmas celebrations. There are still holly trees in the hedge.

17 Continue ahead up track to first buildings of the village of Corfton. The mound of Corfton Castle will be on your left and an interpretation board in front of it. (There is NO PUBLIC ACCESS to the Corfton Castle mound).

Corfton village

At different times parts of the village were owned by the Foxe family from Bromfield, Baldwins and Stedmans.

The estate cottages in the village and Corfton Hall were rebuilt in brick in the Tudor style by Thomas Lloyd Roberts in the years after 1854. P. G. Holder lived there at one time. Corfton Hall was demolished in 1953.

The large Georgian house on the right (now called Corfton Manor) was formerly the Rectory, home to the Vicars of Diddlebury from about 1450 until the new Vicarage was built behind the Diddlebury school in 1883. During WWII land girls were billeted here.

Further up on the left is Lower House Farm, first mentioned in 1582. At various times members of the Lutley, Baldwin and Foxe families owned or leased it. William Gough leased it when he employed Molly Morgan. When the Holder Estate was sold it became for a time the estate offices of the Church Commissioners.

On the main road, to the left, where there is now a house there used to be a shop. The owner during WII was a keen photographer and when some bombs fell at Sutton he took photographs of the damage, had them made into postcards, and sold them in the shop. It is reported that officials from MI5 appeared, and retrieved them from all his customers.

Corfton Castle (The Mount)

The Castle mound can be seen from the road by the Interpretation Board.

Virtually nothing is known about the history of this castle. The only remains are a roughly circular enclosure of 45m internal diameter, with a rampart rising some 5m above the ditch on the exterior. To the east of this are remains of a quadrangular bailey .

It is possible that the castle was erected as the Normans attacked Wales, or by the de Furchis family, who held the manor as undertenants of the de Lacys in the C12 and C13.

The de Lacy family

Ilbert de Lacy came over with William in 1066. Roger held land under the Earl of Montgomery. He was granted Stokesay, but little is known about any buildings that were there then. The Earls of Lincoln are descended from him.

Life in Motte and Bailey Castles

These were primarily garrisons, useful both for defence of an area and to control the local population. Most of the inhabitants were soldiers, which meant cavalry in the Marches. There were also servants, cooks and grooms, and tradesmen such as blacksmiths and farriers. There were some women too.

    The building on top of the motte was usually a two-storeyed round tower. The senior soldiers slept in the lower storey, and the commander of the castle, with his family if he had them with him, on the upper floor. A balcony or walkway projected from this upper floor to serve as a lookout.

    In the bailey there was stabling for the horses, barracks of some sort for the men, and barns for storing grain and fodder. There were also sheds if any ploughing oxen were kept, and kitchens, bakeries and workshops. The roofs were thatched, once the first harvest provided straw.

    Soldiers patrolled the local area regularly, others were occupied in ploughing and growing the essential grain, or supervising the locals to ensure they provided sufficient food for the garrison.

Chapel

Close to the castle is the former chapel of St. Bartholomew. What remains is 9m by 6m, a simple rectangle, but a drawing dated 1790 shows an extra chancel and bell tower.

    An earlier chapel was in existence before 1260, but in 1635 was declared ruinous. The Vicar of Diddlebury and the Corfton inhabitants were held liable to pay for repairs. Tradition says that the existing building was built in the C18 for the convenience of an old man who refused to go to the parish church. It was used at least until the end of the C18, and several marriages were celebrated there, including William Gough's first marriage in 1774. It fell rapidly into ruin later,

parts of it and the bell tower disappearing altogether, and is now part of Hill Farm buildings. *(This is NOT OPEN TO THE PUBLIC.)*

If you divert to the main road there is the Sun Inn.

The Sun Inn

Dating from the C17, it was known as the Sun from 1758. Licenced in 1770, this is one of the oldest Inns in the area.

The Infamous Molly Morgan

On the 31st January 1762 Mary (known as Molly) Jones was baptised at Diddlebury. She lived in a cottage behind the Sun Tavern, Corfton, where her father David was an odd job man for the landlord, John Maebury, and also a fox catcher for which he received a shilling per head.

William Gough lived at Lower House Farm, and was one of the main farmers in the district. When his wife died in April 1778 Molly went to look after his two young children. Five years later Molly had a baby daughter, and the father was presumed to be Gough. He seems to have paid maintenance for the child, Mary. In 1784 Gough married again, and a year later Molly married William Morgan, an apprentice wheelwright and carpenter with Thomas Pinches of Bache Mill. They lived with her parents at Corfton for a while, had a son James, then moved to Cold Weston.

In 1789 some hempen yarn laid out for bleaching vanished, and was found at Molly's house. Both were arrested, but William escaped. Molly was imprisoned in a room at the Sun where she tried to cut her throat. William was captured in Montgomeryshire, but once more escaped when some soldiers intervened.

Molly was found guilty and sentenced to death, but this was commuted to fourteen years' transportation. She was sent to Australia on a ship where conditions were so bad that during the four-month voyage a third of the convicts died, and three quarters of those who survived were sick on arrival. 502 convicts had been crammed into cages, less than two metres square, ten per cage. They were shackled, starved, and rarely permitted on deck.

Somehow William Morgan was also in Australia, and they may have lived together and kept a shop in Parametta, near Sydney. In 1794 Molly escaped and returned to England. She took her children to London, where she met and married Thomas Mears, bell founder and whitesmith of Plymouth. She soon left him, having been accused of trying to set fire to his house.

Back to London, described as the wife of George Meares, labourer, of Southwark, she was convicted in 1803 of the theft of a shift petticoat, napkin and handkerchief and sentenced to seven years' transportation. Molly was again in Parametta. Meanwhile William Morgan had remarried in Australia and with a new family had no more to do with her.

In 1814 she was sentenced by a Convict Settlement Court to another seven years for having some government cattle mixed with her own. By 1819 Molly was in a new settlement at Wallis Plains, on the Hunter River, and in 1822, now aged sixty-one, she married Thomas Hood, aged thirty-one. They prospered, buying more land, and opening the first licenced house for the accommodation of gentlemen and travellers in the White Plains area.

Whatever the truth of the reported thefts, she was highly regarded in Australia. She gave £100 towards building a school. She also visited the sick, ran a home-made hospital, helped settlers, and took special interest in the welfare of convicts, including riding to Sydney to save the lives of convicts accused of stealing fruit. She was reputed to be able to ride, shoot, build fences, dig drains and construct dams better than any man. Wallis Plains was often called Molly Morgan's Plain. She died in 1835 at the age of seventy-three, known as the Queen of Hunter Valley.

Geology from Corfton to Diddlebury

There are lengths of the walk near Diddlebury and Lower Corfton where the soil is of a darker greyish hue. These 'gley' soils have transformed by prolonged water logging.

   The alluvial soils nearest to the streams are less sticky to boots because they contain more sand and less clay particles than the soils on the sloping ground in this part of the walk.

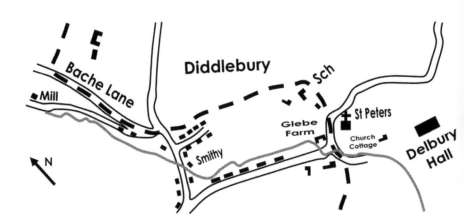

Spectacular Flora

Three magnificent specimens of the Black Poplars (Populus nigra - subspecies betulifolia) can be seen in Lower Corfton. There are a few more within sight of this part of the walk.

   These huge deciduous trees, while so rare as to be classified as endangered elsewhere in England, are a feature of this area, having been planted extensively by landowners in the C19 and early C20.

The old

The new

18 *On the bend where the tarmac starts, go sharp right through two metal kissing gates (between houses) then diagonally*

right across field to stile; cross over farm track and diagonally right again across next field, bear right through metal pedestrian gate, then after 30 yards left through another metal gate.

19 Bear slightly right across parkland, crossing the tarmac drive to Delbury Hall, aiming for Diddlebury Church when that comes into view, to cross a double stile in the hedge opposite; continue down bank and to stile and bridge over stream, then along track through gate to road.

Diddlebury

The name comes from the old English byrig which means stronghold or manor of Dudela, an old English name. The name of the village has undergone many variations of spelling. Before the Norman conquest it was part of Corfham Manor, belonging to Edward the Confessor. Afterwards it was given to Roger, Earl of Montgomery, and by him to Shrewsbury Abbey.

Later the Abbey of Seez in Normandy claimed the lands, on the grounds that Earl Roger had given them several other estates. The church was in the Hereford Diocese, so for almost two hundred years the advowson (presentation of the living) and other rights were disputed by the Abbeys of Seez and Shrewsbury and the Bishop of Hereford. In 1283 the Bishop of Hereford was appointed to arbitrate and gave these rights to Hereford.

It is a large parish with a dozen villages and hamlets, including Corfton, Peaton, Bouldon (since 1881), and Broncroft on the route of the walk; Sparchford, Lawton, Little and Great Sutton nearby, and Westhope to the north west.

As part of Corfham manor the Cliffords held Diddlebury for a time. By the end of the C14 the Baldwin family became important and gradually took over ownership. At the end of the C18 Frederick Cornewall bought the manor. There are memorials in the church to these families, and to the Powells, who held the manor of Little Sutton for several hundred years. There is also a memorial to John Green, schoolmaster for forty years, who died in 1807, lived in Church Cottage beside the churchyard, and who may have taught Molly Morgan to read and write.

The Cornewalls

They were a branch of the family who were barons of Burford.
Humphrey was Sheriff of Herefordshire in 1612. One grandson,
Charles, was a vice-Admiral, the other, Frederick, Vicar of Bromfield for
46 years. Two generations later another Charles was Speaker of the
Commons. Another C18 Cornewall was MP for Ludlow, with a brother
who was Bishop of, in turn, Bristol, Hereford and Worcester.

Old houses in Diddlebury

Delbury Hall, once a home of
the Baldwyn family, was rebuilt
by the Cornewalls in 1752 with
a plain brick frontage, but it
includes an older house at the
back. There was formerly a
malthouse there. During WWII
ammunition was stored on the
estate, and there was a short
stretch of railway in the
grounds. Now there is a
garden centre and trout
fishery.

Delbury is another version
of Diddlebury, and the village's
name is often pronounced this
way by locals.

Glebe Farm, a C17 timber-
framed house stands opposite
the church on the site of the
former residence of the clergy,
used as such until the C15. It
then became a farm, but at
one time it might have been a mill. One was mentioned in 1366.
Behind it is a tithe barn, recently converted into a house.

*To see the front of it you can divert a short way along Mill Lane (straight
on beside the stream from where the path comes out on the road).*

20 *Turn right along elevated
    pavement and at corner,
    cross road to approach to
    village hall/school. Through gate to right of village hall and over stiles
    diagonally across school field.*

St Peter's

St. Peter's Church has some late Saxon
work: the nave; the north wall of this
and parts of the north and west walls of
the tower; a blocked north doorway with
a smaller, round-headed door visible; a
small window in the north wall of the
nave, and herringbone work on the
inside of the north wall.

The Chancel is mainly Norman,
though there is possible Saxon work on
the quoins, and there may have been an
earlier Saxon chancel.

At the end of the C12 the tower was
partly rebuilt, with its archway into the
nave. In the C13 the south aisle was
added to the nave, and in the C14
several windows were inserted, perhaps
two more in the C15. Over the centuries
there have been considerable repairs. In the early C17 the aisle
containing the Cornewall manuments was built, and in the C19 various
repairs were made. The south wall and roof are C19 and in 1884 the
porch was erected.

The original Saxon tower has been rebuilt many times (note the
various buttresses) and has a pair of sheila na-gig fertility images

immediately below the string course of the south wall.

21 *Pass to right of the school building and cross double stile, continue
over two further stiles (with village houses on left) and through gate to
road.*

Bache Mill House

This is a short way to the left along the main road. There was a smithy
here, in use for several centuries, on the west of the stream and south of
the main road. The smithy had collapsed before 1966. Originally there
was a ford north of the present bridge (on which a Tablet was erected
MDCCCL). A tithe map of 1845 shows the ford and footbridge to the
south. There used to be a stone barn where the bungalows were built in
1979.

The house is C17, was enlarged in both the late C18, and early
C19. Three rooms, a dairy, cool store and shop were added. By 1976
there was no longer a dairy or shop, and the exterior door to the shop
was blocked up. At some point the house was also a Post Office, judging
by the blocked letter chute in the wall.

In the C18 and C19 there was a blacksmith and smallholding.
Originally part of the Corfham estate, the tenants bought it in 1921,
when the forge was still working.

There is no evidence of a mill here, but it is possible there was a mill
race about 500m upstream, past the ford on the narrow road which dips
to the left of the route.

Smithies were frequent along the main road, and later, in the days
of the car, many became garages. One garage next to the Sun is now a
private house.

Bache Mill hamlet is on the higher road, along the route, and parts
of it were known as Liverpool and Birmingham.

22 *Turn right, keeping to pavement and in a few yards cross road (with
great care) and up lane to left.*

23 *In approx. 700 yards turn right through gate (opposite converted
former chapel), along field boundary to stile and then diagonally right
across field to another stile at sunken lane.*

24 *Cross sunken lane, over stile at far side, across several fields and two
private drives, then another field to a stile opposite. Descend sunken*

track (can be very slippery) which becomes a lane and down to T-junction. Turn left and in 100 yards reach five-ways junction. Turn right back down to car park.

The final stretch

The path goes round Milford Lodge, built around 1914, then passes below Aston Hall. (NO PUBLIC ACCESS.)

Aston Hall

This is a mid C17 stone-built residence. It is H shaped, but has a jutting central two-storey porch which gives it the appearance of the typical E shape. There are signs of an earlier timber-framed building having been incorporated into the new house.

John Smith, a baron of the Exchequer, owned the manor in 1542, and his descendants, originally from Wootton Wawen in Warwickshire, owned it until 1911 when it was sold to P. G. Holder. He sold it in 1942 to the Church Commissioners, and since then it has become a private residence.

***

APPENDIX

ENGLISH KINGS, THE WELSH AND THE MARCHES

700-600 BC	Many hillforts were constructed, and about 600 survive (20% of the British total are in the area).
200 BC-100 AD	Wales divided into tribal areas, the Cornovii in the central borders.
48 AD	Romans began attacking Wales.
by 80 AD	Romans had conquered Wales.
400 AD	Beginning of Romano-Welsh princedoms as Roman rule dying out.
mid 600s	Anglo-Saxons had reached the Severn, then a natural part of the boundary, and killed Cynddylan, the last Welsh Prince to rule the Shrewsbury area.

A century of border wars followed.

784-796	Offa's Dyke built to define the border area, though it wasn't a fortification and did not stop border wars.

Smaller princedoms amalgamated.

ANGLO-SAXON MONARCHS

802-839	**Egbert, King of Wessex**
839-856	**Ethelwulf**
856-860	**Ethelbald**
860-866	**Ethelbert**
866-871	**Ethelred I**
870-950	Large parts of Wales unified under Rhodri the Great and Hywel the Good.
871-899	**Alfred the Great**
899-924	**Edward the Elder**
924-940	**Athelstan**
940-946	**Edmund I the Elder**
946-955	**Edred**

955-959	**Edwy**	
959-975	**Edgar**	
975-979	**Edward the Martyr**	
979-1013	**Ethelred II the Unready** (deposed)	
1013-1014	**Sweyn Forkbeard, King of Denmark**	
1014-1016	**Ethelred II the Unready**	
1016 (April-Nov)	**Edmund II Ironside**	
1016-1035	**Canute**	
1037-1040	**Harold I Harefoot**	
1040-1042	**Hardicanute**	
1042-1066	**Edward the Confessor**	
	1057-1063	Wales united for the first time by Grufudd ap Llewelyn.
	1063	English invasion left Welsh divided.
1066 (Jan-Oct)	**Harold II**	
1066 (Oct-Dec)	**Edgar Atheling**	

THE NORMANS

1066-1087	**William the Conqueror**	
	1069	Edric the Wild attacks Shrewsbury. Rebellion crushed and county devastated.
	1070	Roger de Montgomery (Later Earl of Shrewsbury) granted much land in county.
	1074	Marcher Lordships established under Earls of Chester, Hereford and Shrewsbury.
	1090-1095	The fiercest period of Norman attacks.
	late C11 & C12	Normans, mainly the Marcher lords, attacked Wales, aided by mail-clad knights. The Normans fought through river valleys, erecting motte and bailey castles as they went. Many soon abandoned as invasion progressed, but some strengthened by stone buildings.

The Welsh fought back and by about 1105 an uneasy balance was arrived at.

Wales again fragmented, and many independent Marcher Lords, so Border battles continued.

1087-1100	**William II (Rufus)**	

1098	Robert de Belleme becomes Earl
1100-1135	**Henry I (Beauclerk)**
1102	Robert rebels, deprived of earldom.
1114	Fitz Flaalds, who become the Fitz Alans, become powerful.
1120	Welsh raids
1135-1154	**Stephen**
	Matilda (died 1167)

Disputed succession. At first Ludlow and Shrewsbury castles held for Matilda.

THE PLANTAGENETS

1154-1189	**Henry II**
1154/5	Hugh de Mortimer rebellion. Cleobury Castle taken and destroyed by King.
1189-1199	**Richard I (Coeur de Lion)**
1195/6	Clun burnt by Welsh
1199-1216	**John (Lackland)**
1200	Llewelyn the Great succeeds to Gwynedd. He was married to King John's illegitimate daughter. His strength threatened Marcher territory.
1211	Llewellyn starts war against the King.
1215	Magna Carta.
1216	Civil War starts.
1216-1272	**Henry III**
1218-1240	Llewelyn dominates Wales, and the only leader entitled to be called 'Prince'.
1220	King meets Llewellyn at Shrewsbury to guarantee right of son David to succeed him
1232 and 1234	Welsh capture Shrewsbury.
by 1258	Llewelyn ap Gruffud, his grandson, known as Llewelyn the Last, had re-established supremacy of Gwynedd, receives oaths of homage and allegiance from Welsh chieftains.
1267	After intervening in the civil wars between Henry III and the barons, he was recognised by the Treaty of Montgomery. Llewelyn acknowledged as Prince of Wales, rules 75% of it, and

	threatens Marchers, who responded by building stronger castles, often with round keeps.
1267	Peace with David ap Llewellyn concluded.
1272-1307	**Edward I**
1277	King conquers Wales.
1277	Edward I sent largest medieval army gathered in Britain into Wales when Llewelyn did not recognise him as overlord. Llewellyn left with a smaller Gwynedd. Edward built many strong castles.
1282-83	Edward I invaded again and Llewelyn killed at Cilmeri, near Builth.
1283	David ap Gruffyd executed at Shrewsbury. Assembly of magnates at Shrewsbury and Acton Burnell.
1284	Edward I's son born at Caernarvon.
1291	Licence to Crenellate granted to Laurence de Ludlow for Stokesay.
1301	First English 'Prince of Wales' created.

As threats of Welsh rebellions seemed over, less-fortified homes such as comfortable manor houses built.

1307-1327	**Edward II**
1327-1377	**Edward III**
1348/9	Black Death
1377-1399	**Richard II**
1399-1413	**Henry IV**
1400-1415	Owen Glendwr's rebellion. During this time local Welshmen again controlling their own areas, and later on absent English landlords often used Welsh deputies, frequently men they had fought alongside in the French wars.
1413-1422	**Henry V**
1422-1461	**Henry VI**
1455-1485	Wars of the Roses, Welshmen fought on both sides.
1459	Ludlow Castle plundered.
1461-1470	**Edward IV**
1475	Council of Wales and the Marches established at Ludlow Castle.

1470-1471	**Henry VI (restored)**
1471-1483	**Edward IV (restored)**
1483 (April-June)	**Edward V**
1483-1485	**Richard III**
1485	Henry Tudor, descended through Owen Tudor from Rhodri the Great, crowned King of England.

THE TUDORS

1485-1509	**Henry VII**
1509-1547	**Henry VIII**
1536/9	Dissolution of the Monasteries.
1536-1543	Acts of Union created Welsh unity and gave Wales the modern boundaries. For first time represented in Parliament.
1536	Act of Union, Marcher Lords lose ancient privileges.
1542	Council of Wales and the Marches reconstituted.
1547-1553	**Edward VI**
1553 (July)	**Lady Jane Grey**
1553-1558	**Mary**
1558-1603	**Elizabeth I**

THE STUARTS

1603-1625	**James I**
1625-1649	**Charles I**
1642/8	Civil War
1642-48	During Civil Wars many castles destroyed in sieges or 'slighted' - partially destroyed - afterwards by Parliamentarians.
1645	Shrewsbury taken by Parliamentary forces
1651	Battle of Worcester.
1649-1685	**Charles II**
1660	Monarchy restored.
1685-1689	**James II**
1689-1694	**Mary and William III**
1694-1702	**William III**
1702-1714	**Anne**

THE HOUSE OF HANOVER

1714-1727	**George I**
1727-1760	**George II**
1760-1820	**George III**
1820-1830	**George IV**
1830-1837	**William IV**

THE HOUSE OF SAXE-COBURG & GOTHA

1837-1901	**Victoria**
1901-1910	**Edward VII**

THE HOUSE OF WINDSOR

1910-1936	**George V**
1914-18	World War I
1936 (Jan-Dec)	**Edward VIII**
1936-1952	**George VI**
1939	Start of WWII
1945	End of War
1952-	**Elizabeth II**